Unlock the World of Remote Work

Freight Dispatcher Full Course - Your Ticket to $500 a Week Anywhere

Copyright Page

© 2024 by Vital Life Voyage. All rights reserved.

No part of this book may be reproduced, stored in a retrieval system, or transmitted in any form or by any means, electronic, mechanical, photocopying, recording, scanning, or otherwise, except as permitted under Section 107 or 108 of the 1976 United States Copyright Act, without the prior written permission of the publisher.

This book is protected under the copyright laws of the United States of America. Any reproduction or unauthorized use of the material or artwork contained herein is prohibited without the express written consent of the publisher.

This book is intended solely for informational and educational purposes. It should not be used as a substitute for professional, financial, or legal advice. The author and publisher make no representations or warranties of any kind, express or implied, about the book's completeness, accuracy, reliability, suitability, or availability or the information, products, services, or related graphics contained in the book for any purpose. Therefore, any reliance placed on such information is strictly at your own risk.

This book may include affiliate links. The author may receive a commission for purchases made through these links. However, the content or recommendations made in this book is acceptable. The author only includes affiliate links for products or services that they believe will add value to the reader.

Please consult with a professional advisor or attorney before making any financial decisions based on the content of this book. The author and publisher are not responsible for errors, inaccuracies, or omissions. They shall not be liable for any loss or damage of any kind, including, but not limited to, any direct, indirect, incidental, consequential, special, or exemplary damages arising from or in connection with the use of this book or its information.

Published by Vital Life Voyage

www.vitallifevoyage.store

vitallifevoyage@gmail.com

Printed in the United States of America

Table of Contents

Chapter 1: Understanding the U.S.A Trucking Industry	4
Chapter 2: 10 Steps to Loading a Truck	7
Chapter 3: ELD Mandate and Hours of Service	9
Chapter 4: Market Analysis and How to Load a Carrier at Top Rates	11
Chapter 5: How to Book Loads Better Than Your Neighbor	13
Chapter 6: Dispatcher's Problems and How to Solve Them	15
Chapter 7: Finding a Job as a Dispatcher	18
Chapter 8: How to Find Customers and Start Your Own Business Without Investment	20
Chapter 9: How to Get Access to Full Video Course	22
Chapter 10: Finale	23

Chapter 1: Understanding the U.S.A Trucking Industry

Introduction

Welcome to "Unlock the World of Remote Work: Freight Dispatcher Full Course - Your Ticket to $500 a Week Anywhere." In our swiftly transforming digital epoch, conventional work paradigms are being revolutionized. The ascent of remote work has unfurled an expanse of opportunities, empowering individuals to generate income from virtually any location with internet connectivity.

This time aspires to be your compass to one of the most auspicious and remunerative remote vocations: freight dispatching. Whether you seek a malleable occupation that aligns with your lifestyle or aim to amplify your earnings, stepping into the role of a freight dispatcher presents a thrilling venture into the burgeoning logistics sector.

In this prelude, we shall unveil a glimpse into the realm of freight dispatching and underscore the myriad advantages it proffers. Nevertheless, it is imperative to recognize that this introduction merely skims the surface. To truly hone the expertise required to excel in this domain and unleash its full potential, delving into the extensive training encapsulated in the full course is indispensable.

If your aspiration is to evolve into a proficient freight dispatcher and optimize your financial prospects, we exhort you to engage with the complete package delineated within these pages. Conversely, if you are keen to expedite your journey and commence earning posthaste, proceed directly to Chapter 9, where you will discover how to access the ten free lessons bonus video course and Chapter 10 to decide to change your life, with 3000 students enrolled the complete practical course: 10 sections • 45 lectures • 7h 38m total length.

The U.S. trucking sector forms the backbone of the nation's economic structure, ferrying commodities from one coast to another and significantly contributing to global supply chains. Excelling as a remote freight dispatcher necessitates a profound understanding of the principal entities, regulatory frameworks, and prevailing trends within this sphere.

Principal Entities in the U.S.A. Trucking Domain:

Carriers: These entities possess fleets of trucks and undertake the transportation of goods for shippers. Carriers range from extensive fleets comprising hundreds of trucks to modest independent operators.

Shippers: Shippers are enterprises requiring the transportation of their merchandise. They engage carriers to transfer their products from distribution hubs to retail locations or directly to consumers.

Brokers: Brokers function as intermediaries between shippers and carriers, aiding shippers in locating trucks for their freight and assisting carriers in securing loads to transport.

Dispatchers: Dispatchers orchestrate the movement of trucks, ensuring timely delivery of freight. They liaise with drivers, shippers, and recipients to plan routes and schedule pickups and drop-offs.

Regulatory Frameworks Impacting the Trucking Sector:

ELD Mandate: The Electronic Logging Device (ELD) mandate compels commercial drivers to employ electronic logging devices to accurately record their hours of service (HOS). This regulation aims to enhance safety and mitigate driver fatigue by ensuring adherence to HOS rules.

Hours of Service (HOS) Regulations: HOS regulations delineate the permissible on-duty and driving hours for drivers. These rules are designed to prevent accidents stemming from driver fatigue by setting caps on driving hours and mandating rest intervals.

Trends Sculpting the Future of Trucking:

Technology Integration: The trucking industry is progressively adopting technology to bolster efficiency and safety. Innovations such as GPS tracking and real-time freight visibility platforms are revolutionizing the management and movement of freight.

Shift Towards Sustainability: Growing environmental sustainability concerns are prompting numerous trucking firms to invest in alternative fuels and cleaner technologies to curtail emissions and diminish their environmental footprint.

Grasping these fundamental aspects of the U.S. trucking sector establishes the foundation for thriving as a remote freight dispatcher. In subsequent chapters, we will explore the requisite skills and strategies to excel in this dynamic and gratifying field

Chapter 2: 10 Steps to Loading a Truck

Loading a truck with efficiency is crucial for optimizing productivity and ensuring punctual deliveries. This chapter elucidates ten meticulous steps to load a truck with precision:

Anticipate and Strategize: Prior to commencing the loading process, evaluate the shipment's dimensions, mass, and delicacy. Devise a loading sequence that optimizes spatial use and mitigates the risk of damage.

Streamline the Dock: Ensure that the loading dock is uncluttered and systematically arranged. Segregate incoming and outgoing consignments to avert confusion and expedite the loading procedure.

Employ Appropriate Apparatus: Utilize suitable equipment, such as forklifts, pallet jacks, and loading ramps, to maneuver freight onto the truck with safety and efficiency.

Strategic Stacking: Stack freight with security in mind, positioning heavier items at the base and lighter ones atop. Employ pallets and load bars to avert shifting during transit.

Equitable Weight Distribution: Distribute weight uniformly across the truck to maintain stability and avert axle overloading. Heed axle weight limits and adjust the load accordingly.

Secure the Freight: Utilize straps, chains, and dunnage to secure the load and prevent displacement during transit. Verify that all cargo is firmly secured before sealing the trailer doors.

Clear Labeling: Label each shipment distinctly with its destination and handling instructions. Clear labeling diminishes the risk of errors and ensures seamless delivery at the final destination.

Space Maximization: Optimize the available space by filling gaps with smaller items or using load bars to create additional tiers. Maximize cubic capacity without breaching weight constraints.

Document the Load: Maintain accurate records of the loaded freight, detailing item descriptions, quantities, and special handling requirements. This documentation facilitates tracking and tracing shipments.

Pre-Departure Inspection: Conduct a final inspection of the loaded truck to confirm everything is secure and complies with regulations. Verify that the trailer doors are securely closed and sealed.

By adhering to these ten steps, you can load a truck safely, efficiently, and in compliance with industry standards. Proficient loading practices lead to timely deliveries, satisfied clients, and a flourishing career in freight dispatching.

Chapter 3: ELD Mandate and Hours of Service

The Electronic Logging Device (ELD) mandate and Hours of Service (HOS) regulations are critical aspects of the trucking industry that every dispatcher must understand. In this chapter, Within the realm of the trucking industry, the Electronic Logging Device (ELD) mandate and Hours of Service (HOS) regulations are pivotal elements that every dispatcher must comprehend.

The ELD Mandate

The Federal Motor Carrier Safety Administration (FMCSA) implemented the ELD mandate, requiring commercial drivers to use electronic logging devices to record their hours of service.

ELDs automatically track driving time, engine hours, vehicle movement, and location data.

Impact on Drivers and Carriers

For drivers, ELDs simplify record-keeping and help ensure compliance with HOS regulations.

Hours of Service (HOS) Regulations

HOS regulations govern the maximum amount of time drivers can spend on-duty and driving before they are required to take a rest break.

Key HOS regulations include:

- **11-Hour Driving Limit:** Drivers may drive a maximum of 11 hours after 10 consecutive hours off-duty.

- **14-Hour Duty Limit:** Drivers may not drive beyond the 14th consecutive hour after coming on duty, following 10 hours off-duty.

- **30-Minute Rest Break:** Drivers must take a 30-minute break after 8 hours of driving time.

- **70-Hour/8-Day Limit:** Drivers may not drive after accumulating 70 hours of on-duty time in any 8-day period.

Chapter 4: Market Analysis and How to Load a Carrier at Top Rates

To succeed as a freight dispatcher, it's essential to understand market dynamics and know-how to secure top-paying loads for carriers.

Market Analysis Techniques:

Identify Demand: Stay informed about industry trends and market demand for freight transportation.

Research Rates: Research prevailing freight rates for different lanes and types of cargo. Online load boards, industry publications, and freight rate indices can provide valuable insights into market pricing.

Assess Competition: Understand your competitors, including other dispatchers, brokers, and carriers operating in your target market. Analyze their pricing strategies, service offerings, and customer base to identify opportunities for differentiation.

Build Relationships: Cultivate relationships with shippers, carriers, and brokers to access exclusive freight opportunities and negotiate favorable rates. Networking and maintaining a strong reputation for reliability and professionalism can open doors to lucrative partnerships.

Strategies for Securing Top-Paying Loads:

Offer Value-Added Services: Differentiate yourself by offering value-added services such as expedited shipping, specialized handling, or dedicated capacity.

Optimize Routing: Utilize routing software and real-time data to optimize routes and minimize empty miles. By maximizing efficiency and reducing fuel costs, you can offer competitive rates while maintaining profitability for carriers.

Negotiate Wisely: Negotiate rates strategically based on market conditions, lane demand, and carrier capacity.

Chapter 5: How to Book Loads Better Than Your Neighbor

Booking loads is a competitive facet of freight dispatching that demands effective communication, negotiation prowess, and keen market awareness. In this chapter, we'll explore techniques to secure loads more efficiently than your competitors, thereby maximizing revenue for carriers.

1. Establish a Strong Online Presence

In the digital era, a robust online presence is essential for attracting clients and securing loads. Maintain an updated website and active social media profiles that highlight your services, showcase testimonials from satisfied customers, and demonstrate your industry expertise.

2. Utilize Load Board Platforms

Leverage load board platforms to access a broad array of available loads and connect with shippers and brokers. Set up alerts for relevant freight opportunities and proactively bid on or negotiate rates for desirable loads.

3. Develop Relationships with Shippers and Brokers

Fostering strong relationships with shippers and brokers can lead to repeat business and exclusive load opportunities. Dedicate time to networking, attending industry events, and providing exceptional service to earn their trust and loyalty.

4. Offer Flexible Solutions

Be adaptable and accommodating when working with shippers and carriers to meet their specific needs. Offer solutions such as partial truckloads, expedited shipping, or specialized handling to distinguish yourself from competitors and secure more business.

5. Provide Excellent Customer Service

Deliver outstanding customer service throughout the booking process, from initial inquiry to final delivery. Promptly respond to inquiries, provide accurate information, and proactively communicate any updates or issues to build trust and confidence with your customers.

6. Leverage Technology

Utilize technology tools such as transportation management systems (TMS), load tracking software, and electronic document management to streamline the booking process and offer shipment visibility to both shippers and carriers.

By implementing these strategies, you can enhance your booking success rate and outperform competitors in the highly competitive freight dispatching market. In the next chapter, we'll tackle common problems faced by dispatchers and offer effective solutions

Chapter 6: Dispatcher's Problems and How to Solve Them

As a freight dispatcher, you'll encounter various challenges in your daily operations. In this chapter, we'll discuss common problems faced by dispatchers and provide effective solutions to overcome them.

1. Communication Issues

Problem: Inefficient communication can lead to misunderstandings, delays, and missed opportunities.

Solution: Implement clear communication protocols and utilize technology tools such as email, phone calls, and messaging apps to ensure timely and accurate information exchange. Establish regular check-ins with drivers, shippers, and carriers to address any issues promptly.

2. Capacity Constraints

Problem: Finding available trucks to meet customer demand can be challenging, especially during peak seasons or in tight capacity markets.

Solution: Develop a network of reliable carriers and maintain open lines of communication to secure capacity when needed. Partner with multiple carriers to increase flexibility and access to available trucks. Explore backhaul opportunities and offer attractive rates to incentivize carriers to accept loads.

3. Freight Scheduling Challenges

Problem: Coordinating pickups and deliveries to meet customer requirements and optimize driver schedules can be complex.

Solution: Utilize scheduling software or transportation management systems (TMS) to efficiently plan and manage freight movements. Prioritize loads based on urgency, proximity, and customer preferences. Communicate proactively with drivers and customers to minimize delays and maximize efficiency.

4. Regulatory Compliance

Problem: Staying compliant with constantly changing regulations, such as the ELD mandate and hours of service rules, can be daunting.

Solution: Stay informed about regulatory updates and invest in training for yourself and your team to ensure compliance. Implement technology solutions, such as ELDs and automated compliance tools, to streamline record-keeping and reduce the risk of violations. Work closely with drivers to educate them on regulations and encourage adherence to safety protocols.

5. Customer Service Issues

Problem: Addressing customer complaints, resolving disputes, and managing expectations can be time-consuming and stressful.

Solution: Prioritize customer service and establish clear processes for handling inquiries, complaints, and requests. Actively listen to customer feedback and take steps to address issues promptly and effectively. Maintain transparency and honesty in all interactions to build trust and foster long-term relationships.

6. Technology Challenges

Problem: Implementing and managing technology solutions can present technical challenges and require ongoing support and training.

Solution: Invest in user-friendly technology platforms and provide comprehensive training for your team to ensure they can effectively utilize the tools. Stay updated on industry trends and advancements in logistics technology to identify opportunities for improvement and innovation.

By addressing these common problems with proactive solutions, you can enhance your effectiveness as a freight dispatcher and deliver exceptional service to your customers and carriers.

Chapter 7: Finding a Job as a Dispatcher

Securing employment as a freight dispatcher necessitates a blend of skills, experience, and industry acumen.

1. **Gain Relevant Experience:** Employers often prefer candidates with prior experience in transportation, logistics, or dispatching. Consider starting in entry-level roles like dispatcher assistant or freight coordinator to acquire valuable skills and familiarity with the industry.

2. **Obtain Training and Certification:** Invest in training programs or certification courses to augment your understanding of dispatching practices, industry regulations, and technology tools. Certifications like the Certified Dispatcher designation can underscore your dedication to professionalism and proficiency.

3. **Network within the Industry:** Networking is instrumental in uncovering job opportunities and forging connections with potential employers. Attend industry gatherings, join professional associations, and engage with professionals in transportation and logistics to broaden your network and discover hidden job prospects.

4. **Customize Your Resume and Cover Letter:** Tailor your resume and cover letter to spotlight pertinent skills, experiences, and achievements that highlight your suitability for a dispatcher role.

5. **Utilize Online Job Boards and Recruitment Platforms:** Explore dispatcher positions on online job boards, industry-specific websites, and recruitment platforms. Tailor your job search criteria to target companies aligning with your career aspirations and preferences.

6. **Prepare for Interviews:** Be ready to delve into your experience, skills, and qualifications during job interviews. Practice responding to common

interview queries and be prepared to furnish examples of how you've navigated challenging scenarios in previous roles.

In the ensuing chapter, we'll explore methods for acquiring customers and initiating your own dispatcher business sans investment.

Chapter 8: How to Find Customers and Start Your Own Business Without Investment

Embarking on your own dispatcher business can be a gratifying endeavor, demanding meticulous planning and strategic implementation. In this chapter, we'll explore methodologies for discovering customers and commencing your dispatcher business sans substantial upfront investment.

1. **Identify Your Target Market:** Pinpoint the customer segments you aim to serve, whether it's small businesses, independent carriers, or specific industries like manufacturing or retail. Understanding your target market will aid in tailoring your marketing endeavors and services to meet their requirements.

2. **Build Your Online Presence:** Craft a professional website and establish a presence on social media platforms like LinkedIn, Facebook, and Twitter. Leverage these channels to exhibit your services, disseminate industry insights, and interact with potential clientele.

3. **Network Effectively:** Participate in industry events, trade shows, and networking gatherings to forge connections with prospective customers and collaborators. Engage with online communities and forums pertinent to transportation and logistics to broaden your network and cultivate relationships with industry peers.

4. **Offer Free Trials or Samples:** Consider offering complimentary trials or samples of your dispatcher services to entice new customers. This affords potential clients the opportunity to experience the value you provide without an initial financial commitment.

5. **Provide Exceptional Service:** Prioritize delivering exceptional customer service to foster trust and loyalty among your clientele. Focus on reliability, communication, and adept problem-solving to ensure a positive experience for every customer interaction.

6. **Utilize Referral Programs:** Incentivize contented customers to refer others to your business by offering rewards such as discounts or credits for future services. Word-of-mouth referrals can serve as a potent means to attract new clients and organically expand your business.

7. **Collaborate with Brokers and Carriers:** Cultivate partnerships with freight brokers and carriers to access a broader clientele base and augment your freight opportunities. By collaborating closely with these industry allies, you can harness their resources and expertise to amplify your business scope.

8. **Leverage Online Platforms:** Harness online load boards, freight marketplaces, and digital platforms to identify and engage with customers seeking dispatcher services. These platforms can furnish valuable leads and avenues for expanding your business sans substantial investment.

9. **Focus on Marketing and Branding:** Dedicate effort to effectively marketing your dispatcher business.

10. **Expand Your Service Offering:** Contemplate diversifying your service portfolio to accommodate the evolving needs of your clientele.

Chapter 9: How to Get Access to Full Video Course

FREIGHT DISPATCHER - 10 FREE LESSONS BONUS CLICK TO LINK BELOW:

https://www.youtube.com/playlist?list=PLp3QmYs-hTikhpL4dfh3n89YNu2Ldtd4v

Scan the following QR Code to get access to the bonus

Chapter 10: Finale

Thank you for reading this introductory book, designed to give you a glimpse into the exciting and lucrative world of freight dispatching. However, what you've read in this book is just the beginning. To truly become a proficient freight dispatcher, equipped with all the necessary tools and materials, I highly recommend you purchase the comprehensive full course.

Why Invest in the Full Course?

By enrolling in the full Freight Dispatcher Course, you will gain access to:

Complete Training: Detailed modules covering every aspect of freight dispatching.

Practical Tools: Essential tools and resources that will enable you to perform your job efficiently.

Certification: Upon completing the course, you will receive a certificate to present to potential employers or clients.

Achieve Your Short-Term Goals

With the full course, you will be equipped to achieve your short-term goals and start earning $500 a week or more. Whether you choose to work for an employer or start your own freight forwarding business, the opportunities are endless.

Start Your Own Business or Secure a High-Paying Job

As a certified freight forwarder, you have the potential to:

Start Your Own Business: Operate as an individual freight forwarder anywhere in the world.

Earn a High Salary: The average salary for a freight forwarder is $2,500 per month or $60,000 per year.

Affordable Investment for a Lucrative Career

The full course is available at a very affordable price, making it a worthwhile investment in your future. By acquiring these in-demand skills, you can unlock the door to financial independence and global mobility.

Just ~~$199~~ - $29!

This comprehensive course equips you with hands-on skills to excel in the US market. Derived from our internal training system, trusted by over 3000 dispatchers, you'll learn practical tools directly applicable to real-world scenarios.

🌟 Bestseller! Rated 4.7/5 (167 ratings) with 3000 students enrolled!

🎓 10 sections • 45 lectures • 7h 38m total length

📚 Freight Dispatcher Full Course - https://pay.hotmart.com/X92936664R